CARLO ACUTIS

CARLO ACUTIS

God's Computer Genius

By Ellen Labrecque

Illustration and design by Dan Wegendt

Pauline
BOOKS & MEDIA
Boston

Library of Congress Control Number: 2021938258

CIP data is available.

ISBN 10: 0-8198-1700-7
ISBN 13: 978-0-8198-1700-6

Illustration and design by Dan Wegendt

A Prayer to Blessed Carlo Acutis contributed by Sr. Allison Gliot

"P" and PAULINE are registered trademarks of the Daughters of St. Paul.

Published by Pauline Books & Media, 50 Saint Pauls Avenue, Boston, MA 02130-3491

Printed in the U.S.A.

CAGCG VSAUSAPEOILL7-110182 1700-7

www.pauline.org

Pauline Books & Media is the publishing house of the Daughters of St. Paul, an international congregation of women religious serving the Church with the communications media.

1 2 3 4 5 6 7 8 9   25 24 23 22 21

Contents

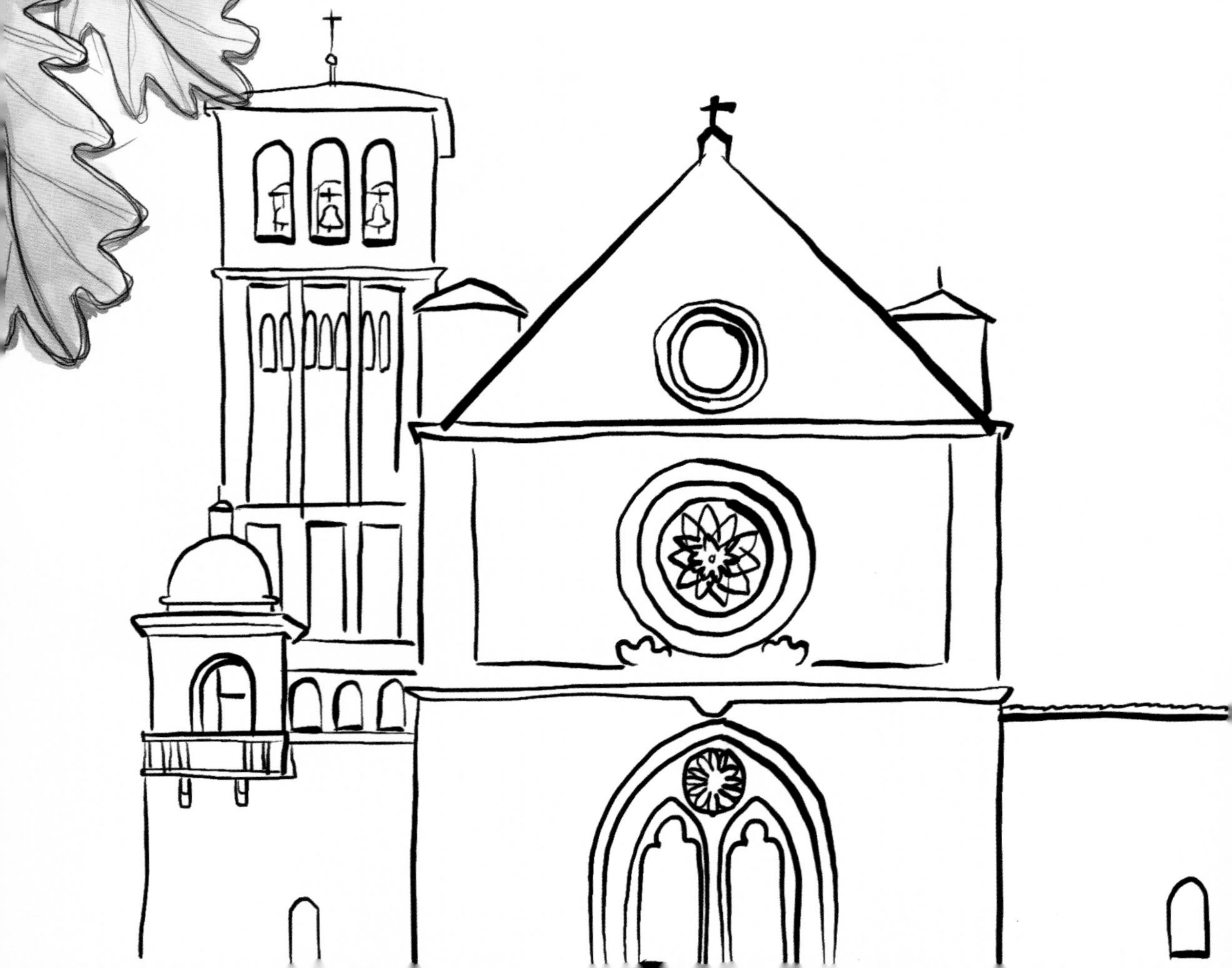

Blessed Carlo

It is a lovely fall day at the Basilica of St. Francis in Assisi, Italy. Carlo Acutis is set to be beatified by the Catholic Church. Carlo died of leukemia—a type of cancer—in 2006 at the age of fifteen. This ceremony on October 10, 2020, is the second-to-last step on the path to sainthood. Carlo could become the first millennial to become a saint in the Church. A millennial is anybody who was born between the years 1981 and 1996. The Catholic Church has declared more than ten thousand people saints, but only a small fraction of them died as children or teenagers. Carlo is special—even among the blessed.

Cardinal Agostino Vallini is presiding over the Mass for Carlo. The Cardinal is a member of the Congregation for the Causes of Saints. This is the group that oversees the process and steps of sainthood. Over three thousand people are in Assisi for the ceremony. In addition to the people in the church, people across the city can watch the Mass on screens that have been set up. Carlo's body is laid in a coffin in the church. He is

dressed in a track jacket, his favorite pair of jeans, and a pair of Nike sneakers.

The next day, Pope Francis, the leader of the Catholic Church, shares how much he admires this young man. "[Carlo] shows today's young people that true happiness is found by putting God first and also by serving our brothers [and sisters], especially the least,"[1] the Pope says.

Carlo Acutis worked to help the poor and always looked out for people in need. But he was also a typical teenager who loved to play video games, write in his journal, hang out with friends, walk his dogs, and use his cellphone. Carlo was a computer wiz who built websites, wrote computer programs, and created graphic and video design.

Carlo didn't just do these things for fun. He used his computer skills as a force for holiness. He brought God and faith to people by using the Internet.

"Carlo was the light answer to the dark side of the web," said Carlo's mother, Antonia. "My son's life can show how the Internet can be used for good—to spread good things."[2]

So why is this exceptional modern teenager on the path to sainthood? This is Carlo's journey.

CHAPTER 1

A Kid Named Carlo

Carlo Acutis was born on May 3, 1991, in London, England. Both his parents, though, were Italian. His mother was Antonia Salzano Acutis and his father was Andrea Acutis. The family lived in England because Andrea was temporarily working there in business.

Carlo was Antonia and Andrea's first child. Their son was baptized on May 18, just fifteen days after he was born. He was baptized by Father Nicholas Martin in Our Lady of Dolours Church in London. A couple months after the Baptism, Carlo's family moved back to their home city and country, Milan, Italy.

Carlo's mother and father were both Catholic. But they were not devout. This means they didn't go to weekly Mass and they didn't pray daily. In fact, on the day her son was born, Antonia had only been to church three times in her life. She went on the day of her own Baptism, on the day of her Confirmation, and on the day of her wedding. Still, when the family moved back to Italy, they joined the Santa Maria Segreta Parish in

Italy

Italy is a country in Europe that is shaped like a boot. It is one of the most Catholic countries in Europe. Over 78 percent of people there identify themselves as this religion. The capital and largest city in Italy is Rome. Inside of Rome is Vatican City. Vatican City is the smallest country in the world. It is the home of the pope and the headquarters of the Catholic Church.

Milan. They became members of the parish, even if they did not plan on attending Mass. Being Catholic was their identity as much as their religious belief.

Carlo had a nanny named Beata. She helped care for Carlo. Beata was from Poland and was very religious. She would share some of her beliefs with Carlo while she cared for him. "Beata was one of the first people to speak to Carlo about God,"[3] Antonia said.

Carlo was a beautiful baby and grew into a handsome little boy. He had deep, soulful brown eyes and a shock of curly brown hair. He also had a bright smile that made everybody around him smile too.

Milan is also an important city in Italy. It is known as Italy's financial headquarters. It is famous for its high fashion and artwork. It is the home of one of the world's most famous paintings—The Last Supper—by Leonardo da Vinci. Da Vinci created this piece between 1495 and 1498. The painting portrays Jesus and his twelve apostles at a long table. It shows Jesus' final meal with his followers before he is crucified.

By the age of three, Carlo loved visiting churches. He could not walk past a church without asking his mother if they could go inside and greet Jesus. This was new to Carlo's mother, but she took her son anyway. Italy has more than one hundred thousand Catholic churches, and Milan is home to a lot of them. When Carlo visited each church, he liked to put flowers in front of the statues of Mary. The mother of Jesus had a special place in his young heart.

"I was perplexed by his devotion," said his mom, Antonia. "He was so small and so sure."

Since Antonia wasn't religious, she couldn't believe she had a son who was so touched by God. She wasn't even sure she had the tools to help foster this holiness in her son. She soon realized she was going to have to let Carlo show her his way.

When Carlo was six, he attended the primary school at the Institute of Marcelline Sisters in Piazza Tommaseo. It was a Catholic school run by nuns. Carlo was very smart and did well, although sometimes he chatted and joked with friends when he should have been listening to the teacher. After school, Carlo played football (American soccer). He also rode his bike, watched action films, and learned how to play the saxophone.

4

Carlo was popular and had plenty of buddies. Everybody liked him. He had a kind and calm way about him. He always stood up for and defended kids with disabilities who were being bullied. When a friend's parents were going through a divorce, Carlo invited the boy back to his house to spend time with his family. He understood as a young kid that spending time with people is the most important thing a friend can do.

Carlo's best friend was not a student at his school, though. He considered his guardian

angel as his best friend. Catholics believe that everybody has been given a guardian angel from God. The guardian angel guides and protects each person. Carlo prayed to his guardian angel every day.

Teachers and other adults saw Carlo as unique, or different from other boys his age. They would often say to Carlo's mom, "Madame, your son is special!" But the principal of Carlo's grade school, Sister Miranda, thought he blended in well with his classmates.

"I can say that the greatest miracle I saw in Carlo is that he looked like everyone else," she explained, "without making me think he was holier or more innocent of a child than his peers."[4]

GUARDIAN ANGELS

Angels are intelligent spiritual beings created by God. Guardian angels are given to each person by God. A guardian angel's job is to protect, lead, and pray for us. A guardian angel shepherds us through life, helping to lead us to eternal life. We may pray to our guardian angel for help whenever we want to.

On June 16, 1998, Carlo, age seven, made his first Holy Communion. This was two years earlier than most other kids in Italy received this sacrament. But Carlo was so excited to receive the Eucharist that his family had asked and was given special permission by their church for him to receive this sacrament early. He did not celebrate this milestone with a party, though. Instead, dressed in a long white robe and white shoes, Carlo received

ANGEL OF GOD,
MY GUARDIAN DEAR,
TO WHOM GOD'S LOVE
COMMITS ME HERE,
EVER THIS DAY
BE AT MY SIDE,
TO LIGHT AND GUARD,
TO RULE AND GUIDE.

Communion in a monastery of cloistered sisters. A monastery is a place for silence and reflection. Cloistered nuns spend their days in prayer and physical work. They remain apart from the world so that they can be totally dedicated to God and pray for the needs of everyone. Having Carlo's first Communion at such a holy place made it even more special. Over the entrance to the monastery, the words were written, "God is enough."

CHAPTER 2

Holy Sites

Once Carlo made his first Holy Communion, he began to attend Mass on a daily basis. This is a big commitment for an adult, but for a kid as young as Carlo, it was exceptional. Carlo's family loved to travel. The first thing Carlo did when they arrived at a new place was find the daily Mass schedule of the nearest Catholic church. As Carlo grew, his family began to take trips to holy places. They toured spots in Europe where it is believed Mary, the mother of Jesus, appeared. Carlo thought

MARIAN APPARITIONS

Catholics believe Mary has appeared in different places around the world. The sightings are called apparitions and are usually given names based on the town where the vision was reported. Sometimes it is said Mary appeared just once. Other times she appeared many times over the course of years. Many of these special miracles have been investigated and approved by the Church as being real.

Two of the most famous apparitions were in Lourdes, France, and Fatima, Portugal. A young girl named Bernadette said Mary visited her eighteen times in Lourdes in 1858. Mary revealed a spring to Bernadette that had miraculous healing power. Today, more than six million people visit Lourdes a year. Many are hoping to be healed by taking a dip in the waters.

Mary also appeared to three poor children in Fatima. She spoke to them about the importance of prayer and being sorry for sins, and encouraged them to love Jesus. As many as four million people visit Fatima every year.

of these trips as pilgrimages. A pilgrimage is a trip for spiritual or religious reasons.

As Carlo grew up, he became more and more committed to prayer and his relationship with God. Carlo was also always looking for ways to help people. Carlo's family was very wealthy. His father was an international businessman who was in charge of different companies. But Carlo never cared about money. He never boasted or bragged. He was very humble. If his mom tried to buy him an extra pair of shoes, Carlo would refuse them. He never wanted any more than he really needed.

Even though Carlo's family was rich, the city of Milan had the most homeless people of any city in Italy. Carlo passed many of them on his way to school. Many other kids as young as Carlo might not notice these people in need. But Carlo did. And he felt compassion for the poor. Carlo often talked to them and listened to their problems. He wanted to spread God's kindness and love everywhere.

Carlo soon asked his mother if he could try to help some of the homeless people living in Milan. He began by bringing them hot meals and sleeping bags. He also volunteered in a soup kitchen run by the Missionaries of Charity, a group of religious sisters. A soup kitchen is a place that serves free meals to the homeless and the poor. While working at the

12

soup kitchen, Carlo became especially good friends with Sister Giovanna Negrotto, who helped run the kitchen. Once Carlo asked her the question, "Is God more pleased with a service like this? Or with prayer?" Sister Giovanna answered Carlo that she thought both ways pleased God.

Carlo also loved animals. He had four dogs, two cats, and many goldfish. He often made videos of his dogs playing. Carlo also enjoyed playing video games, especially *Mario Kart* and *Pokémon*. But Carlo wasn't just a casual video game player. He was a bright and curious child. He wanted to understand how video games and computers really worked. One of Carlo's heroes was Steve Jobs. Steve Jobs was a

STEVE JOBS (1955-2011)

Steve Jobs was one of the founders of the company Apple. Apple makes the Macintosh computer as well the iPad and the iPhone. It is one of the most successful companies in the world.

Steve was born in San Francisco, California, on February 24, 1955. As a boy, he loved electronics and spent a lot of his time building and rebuilding things. At the time, personal computers were big, slow, and clunky. Very few people owned them. But Steve believed computers would change the world and that everybody should have a personal computer in their home.

Years after inventing the popular Mac computers, Steve and Apple introduced the iPhone to the world on January 9, 2007. Smartphones put a powerful computer in every person's pocket. Steve was a visionary. This meant he had big ideas about the future and plans for how to change the world.

Steve died of cancer in 2011. He was fifty-six years old.

computer genius who co-founded Apple Computers. Steve Jobs had a famous quote about our time on Earth.

"Your time is limited," Steve Jobs said. "So do not waste it living someone else's life."[5]

Carlo believed this too.

When Carlo was nine years old, he began studying college-level computer science textbooks. He soon taught himself how to code.

Just like Steve Jobs, Carlo was becoming a visionary. But Carlo wasn't planning to use his computer skills to make money or become famous. He had other goals in mind. So even though Carlo loved computers, he was very disciplined. He only allowed himself to play video games for

Coding

Coding is how we talk to computers. A computer can do so many amazing things—like help you with your homework, create cool video games, play music and television shows, and make graphics. But in order for computers to do these things, they have to be told what to do. People who are computer programmers do just that. They give computers a set of instructions to perform tasks. These step-by-step instructions are called coding. And just like people in the world speak different languages, there are hundreds of different coding languages as well.

Computer coding soon became Carlo's passion. He wanted to learn everything about how technology worked. He taught himself several coding languages. He became fluent in ones called C++ and Java, among others.

"He learned how to code in several languages," explained Carlo's mom. "He taught himself everything, including 3-D animation. It was unbelievable."[6]

one hour each week. He did not want them to take up too much of his time. And he always used what he learned to help others. He showed friends and family all the things computers can really do. As he learned, he always tried to teach.

Carlo kept a journal. He wanted to write down the ways he could work to improve himself. Like most children, Carlo loved sweet treats. He especially loved Nutella and ice cream. And although he did allow himself treats, Carlo also made sure he didn't eat too many. Carlo wrote about the importance of moderation in his journal:

"What does it matter if you can win a thousand battles, if you cannot win against your own corrupt passions? The real battle is within ourselves," he would say. Carlo's big vision for his life was to live for Jesus and to remember that he was made for heaven.

3+7=10

CHAPTER 3

Sharing His Faith

When Carlo was eleven, he received the sacrament of Confirmation. In the Catholic Church, this means he received the gifts of the Holy Spirit and was now considered fully initiated in the Church. Carlo's religious journey that began with Baptism was "confirmed." After Carlo made his Confirmation, he began helping to teach religious classes at his church. He created what he called a "Holiness Kit." The kit involved nine steps to practice living your best holy life.

Carlo's Holiness Kit

CARLO CREATED A HOLINESS KIT FOR HIS CATHOLIC STUDENTS TO PRACTICE ON A DAILY BASIS. THE PRACTICES WERE:

— Love God with all your heart
— Go to Mass
— Receive Communion
— Pray the Rosary
— Read a passage of the Bible
— Visit Jesus in the Tabernacle
— Go to confession (weekly)
— Help others as much as you can
— Rely on your guardian angel as your best friend

Carlo also shared his faith at home. His family employed a housekeeper named Rajesh. Rajesh was not Catholic. He was born into a different religion called Hinduism. But he and Carlo formed a special bond with each other. Even though it was Rajesh's job to keep the family's house clean, Carlo did everything he could to make that job easier. Carlo got up early and made his own bed and cleaned his own room so Rajesh would not have to do it for him. The two spent time together. And seeing how strong Carlo's Catholic beliefs were made Rajesh want to be a Catholic too.

"I got baptized a Christian because he electrified me with his faith,"[7] Rajesh explained.

Around this same time, Carlo began his life's work. He had come to understand that the Internet was a powerful tool that connected the world, but it could be used for bad things. It could be used to spread lies and false news. Carlo wanted to use the web totally differently. He wanted to communicate the Good News of the Gospel on this new platform and connect Jesus with a younger generation. He wanted to change the world this way. One person who inspired Carlo to use the Internet in this positive way was a famous Italian priest, Blessed James Alberione.

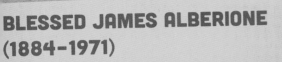

BLESSED JAMES ALBERIONE
(1884-1971)

James Alberione was born in San Lorenzo di Fossano, Italy, on April 4, 1884. He knew he wanted to be a priest by the time he was in first grade. He enrolled in the seminary, a special school where future priests are trained, at the age of sixteen.

Father James modeled his life on the apostle Saint Paul. He wanted to share the Gospel with people just like Paul did. But he wanted to use modern ways of communicating to spread the Catholic faith. Father James started a religious community called the Society of St. Paul in 1914 to do just that. The Pauline Family grew from there. It is now a network of churches, religious orders, and followers that use modern communication tools to spread God's love. Like Carlo, Blessed James wanted to spread good news—especially the Good News of the Gospel of Jesus—not bad news.

The Daughters of St. Paul are the religious sisters who run Pauline Books and Media (the publishers of this book!). The Pauline mission is to give Christ to the world through every possible form of communication. The Daughters of St. Paul, together with many creative and talented collaborators, create books, websites, podcasts, and musical albums, among other things, in order to help people to know the love of Jesus.

Father James died of natural causes in 1971, was made blessed in 1996, and is on his way to officially becoming a saint.

Carlo created a website for his parish in Milan. Other churches in the area soon asked him to do the same for them. Most importantly, Carlo began creating a website about the eucharistic miracles around the world. He truly believed in the importance and power of Jesus' presence

What is a Eucharistic Miracle?

The Eucharist is also called Holy Communion. In the Bible, we read about what Jesus did at the Last Supper: "While they were eating, Jesus took a loaf of bread, and after blessing it he broke it, gave it to the disciples, and said, 'Take, eat; this is my body.' Then he took a cup, and after giving thanks he gave it to them, saying, 'Drink from it, all of you; for this is my blood of the covenant, which is poured out for many for the forgiveness of sins.'" (Mt 26:26–28). Jesus then asked his disciples to do this in his memory. During the Mass, that is exactly what we do. When the priest uses the words of Jesus to consecrate the bread and the wine, we believe Jesus is present to us in his Body, Blood, Soul, and Divinity. This is what we call the Eucharist.

Throughout the history of the Catholic Church, eucharistic miracles have occurred. These miracles are a gift from God to help people understand that the Eucharist really is the real Body and Blood of Christ. Sometimes people have been healed from what were thought to be incurable diseases after receiving Communion. There have even been saints who have miraculously lived and survived on the Eucharist alone! Some of the most well-known eucharistic miracles that have been documented are miracles where the Eucharist actually appears as Jesus' flesh and blood. All of these miracles are meant to help strengthen our faith.

Carlo was fascinated by these miracles. So, when Carlo was just eleven, he began building a website to keep track of them. In order to create this website, Carlo began doing research. He asked his mother if he could visit the different places where the miracles occurred.

in the Eucharist. He wanted to share this belief with everybody. He was trying to connect people of the twenty-first century with God. In this sense, Carlo was a revolutionary. This is a person who tries to change the old ways of doing something and works toward everlasting change. Using three computers, Carlo worked on this website for the next four years.

Carlo believed the Eucharist was powerful.

"The more Eucharist we receive, the more we will become like Jesus," Carlo said.

Carlo read constantly to learn more about his faith. He even read a book about purgatory. Purgatory is the place where people go after they die when they are not yet ready to enter heaven. It helps them prepare for heaven where they will be with Jesus forever. Carlo said he didn't want to go to purgatory. He wanted to go straight to heaven.

"The Eucharist is the highway to heaven," Carlo said.

In 2003, a couple months before Carlo turned twelve, his family took a trip to France to visit Lourdes. This is the place where Mary appeared to Saint Bernadette in 1858. Lourdes has a spring that is believed to be filled with miraculous healing waters. While there, Carlo filled many containers with the spring water. He wanted to bring it home to give to his family and friends. Carlo's favorite dog also joined them on the trip. He was a Chihuahua-terrier mix named Briciola, which means "crumb" in Italian. Carlo took videos of his dog and his family while on this trip. They were such happy days for Carlo. When the family was back home, he continued to teach religious education as well as learn about coding. He gladly shared his knowledge with any friends who asked for him to teach them.

In 2005, when Carlo was fourteen, he entered Leone XIII High School. It was a Catholic high school founded in 1893 by a religious order called the Jesuits. Carlo was a gifted math student. His math teacher remembered that he "was lively and intelligent and had a profound look." Profound means that Carlo seemed to have great wisdom and insight.

Just as he did in grade school, Carlo continued to be a friend to everybody. He always greeted the school's porter, or janitor, with a smile and a wave each morning. Many days he took the time to chat with him for a couple of minutes.

Carlo had a wonderful year at Leone XIII. In addition to math, he studied the classics. This meant he learned the history of the Greeks and the Romans. He was taught about their greatest leaders, artists, writers, and thinkers. He also used his computer skills to create a volunteering page for the school. It listed different organizations and opportunities for

students to give their time to help people in need. He created a program on his computer tracking how he said the Rosary every day. And he continued to work on his website about the eucharistic miracles. He was truly using the Internet as a tool to spread the message of holiness.

THE ROSARY

The Rosary is a series of prayers dedicated to the Virgin Mary. The prayers are recited while holding a string of beads, called a rosary. The rosary has fifty small beads arranged in five sets of ten. These sets are called decades. Each decade has a larger bead that separates the decades. A cross, two large beads, and three smaller ones hold the two ends of the rosary together. A Hail Mary is recited while holding each of the smaller beads. Different prayers, the Glory Be and the Our Father, are then recited while holding the larger beads. While saying each of the decades, one of twenty mysteries are reflected upon. The mysteries are from the life and death of Jesus and Mary. The mysteries are divided into four sets of five, and they are called the Joyful, Sorrowful, Luminous, and Glorious.

Carlo also thought that taking care of the planet was another way to share God's love. Carlo loved to go on walks with his dogs. And when he did walk, he always made a point to pick up garbage wherever he went. He went to the beaches with his mom and swam in the sea. He always tried to pick up garbage in the ocean while swimming. Carlo wanted to be an example of good citizenship. He knew that God created this world and wants us to take good care of it. He believed that living in harmony with the Earth would also help him to live in harmony with God.

While doing this work, Carlo continued to feel an even greater calling to the Catholic Church. He was not thinking about sports and parties. He was always thinking about God and church.

"In Carlo, one could admire a continuous and ever-renewed orientation toward good," said his father, whom he called Papa. "That was possible thanks to his surrender to the Lord."[8]

Even though Carlo was so good, he still believed in going to the sacrament of Reconciliation, or confession, almost weekly. He compared going to confession to a hot air balloon.

"Before it can rise," Carlo said, "a balloon needs to unload the weights. To rise to God, the soul needs to remove the small weights that are sins."[9]

In the summer of 2006, Carlo asked his mom if he should become a priest when he grew up. His mom answered, "You will see it by yourself. God will reveal it to you."

Around that time, Carlo began feeling sick. His entire body ached. He felt tired all the time, even after getting a long night of sleep. He thought he had come down with the flu and just couldn't kick it. By the beginning of the school year, Carlo was still not feeling any better.

The Jesuits are Catholic brothers and priests who belong to the Society of Jesus. Their order was founded in 1534 by Saint Ignatius of Loyola and a group of his friends from the University of Paris. They placed themselves at the service of the pope so that he could send them to wherever the Church was most in need. They started schools all around the world to help people by giving them a good education and teaching them about God.

The Jesuits are still best known today for their work in education. There are more than eight hundred Jesuit high schools and universities around the world. The Jesuits' Latin motto is *Ad Maiorem Dei Gloriam* (AMDG). This translates to "For the greater glory of God." When Jorge Mario Bergoglio became Pope Francis in 2013, he was the first Jesuit priest ever to be named a pope.

CHAPTER 4

Highway to Heaven

On October 9, 2006, Carlo became so ill that he had to check into St. Gerald Hospital, outside of Milan. Carlo was in a lot of pain. After giving him many tests, the doctors soon learned Carlo had advanced stages of leukemia, a deadly cancer. Most people would be devastated by this news. But Carlo looked at his disease in a different way. When he was told of his diagnosis, he smiled and said, "God gave me a beautiful alarm clock."

It was like Carlo already knew his short life on Earth was coming to an end. Instead of being sad, he was able to accept his illness as part of God's plan. Carlo felt happy at the thought of going to heaven because he wanted to be with Jesus forever and see God face to face. Carlo believed death was the start of a new life.

29

The Seven Sacraments

The Catholic Church has seven sacraments, given to us by Jesus. These sacraments are external signs that we can see and hear and touch through which God gives us his grace, which we cannot see! They are

1. Baptism: The priest or deacon pours water on the person (or sometimes they are immersed in water), baptizing the person in the name of the Trinity. Through Baptism, we are cleansed of original sin, are united with Christ, and become a child of God and a member of the Church.

2. Confirmation: Confirmation completes the grace of Baptism, especially deepening the gifts of the Holy Spirit. These strengthen us to live our faith and share it with the world.

3. Eucharist: Refers both to the holy sacrifice of the Mass (in which Jesus renews his offering of himself to the Father), and to the presence of the living Jesus, Body, Blood, Soul, and Divinity (which we receive in Holy Communion).

4. Reconciliation: Through the ministry of the priest, Jesus forgives our sins and reconciles us to the Church. Also called Penance or confession.

5. Anointing of the Sick: Through an anointing with holy oil, those who are seriously sick receive spiritual strength, forgiveness, and sometimes physical healing.

6. Matrimony: Through the sacrament of Matrimony, a baptized man and woman are married. Marriage forms a lifelong covenant of exclusive love, open to bringing children into the world.

7. Holy Orders: This is when a man is ordained a deacon, priest, or bishop. He is given grace and power to serve Christ and the Church, especially by administering the sacraments.

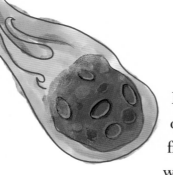

Carlo soon became so weak he couldn't move. He stopped eating or drinking. His death came quickly. On October 10, he received two sacraments from the hospital chaplain. A chaplain is a person who spiritually guides someone, and this one was a Catholic priest. The chaplain, Father Sandro Villa, gave Carlo the Anointing of the Sick and Holy Communion.

"He seemed to have been waiting for [the] sacraments and felt the need for them," said Father Villa about his encounter with Carlo. "I was amazed the Lord allowed me to meet him, if only for a few minutes."[10]

Carlo knew he was going to die soon. His mother and father were devastated. Their only child was so young, and he was going to die before them. For any parent, this was the worst thing that could happen. Carlo just wanted to comfort his mom and dad. He did not even think about himself. Carlo even told his mother that he would give her a sign one day to show he was in heaven with God.

During the night, the nurse who was taking care of Carlo asked if he would like her to go wake up his mother. Carlo responded, "She is very tired as well and will only worry even more."[11] These are thought to be some of the last words Carlo spoke.

The next day, Carlo went into a coma. A coma is like a deep sleep that is caused by

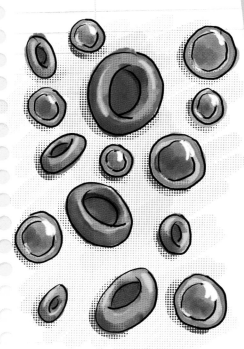

LEUKEMIA

Leukemia is a type of cancer. Cancer is a disease that can happen almost anywhere in the body. It causes cells to grow out of control. These cells destroy other healthy cells and organs in the body.

Leukemia is a cancer that occurs in the blood. The cancer cells that form in the blood make people very sick. They get a fever, their body aches, and they feel very tired all the time. Leukemia can be treated with chemotherapy and radiation. But these treatments are often very difficult on the patient. Doctors still do not know for sure what causes leukemia. And, not everyone who gets leukemia dies from it. But they also do not yet have a permanent cure.

a severe injury or illness. Some patients recover from a coma, but others never wake up. For Carlo, the leukemia had done too much damage to his young body. He died on October 12, 2006, at 6:45 in the morning. He had only been in the hospital for four days. The two doctors that treated him were saddened, but also honored to have met him.

"Carlo was like a meteor with a quick passage through our ward," said one of the doctors. "Leukemia took him away before we could get to know him. However, his sweet eyes remain in our memories."[12]

Carlo's funeral took place in Milan. His friends and fellow students from his Jesuit high school filled the pews. Additionally, many homeless people attended. The crowd spilled out into the street. These were all the people Carlo had made friends with during his short life. Many came and talked with Carlo's mother and father. They told them stories about Carlo's kindness and generosity. Some gave Carlo's mom and dad poems they had written for their son. So many people had been moved by Carlo and his generous spirit. Many of these stories, his mother and father heard for the first time. They had had no idea how many people's lives Carlo had touched.

"It seemed more like a party than a funeral,"[13] said Carlo's mother. She thought the festive atmosphere was because people felt sure Carlo was in heaven.

Saint Francis of Assisi

Saint Francis is one of the most well-known saints in the Catholic Church. He founded a religious order, or group, called the Franciscans. There are Franciscan friars and Franciscan sisters. Friars are religious men who take vows like sisters do and spend their lives preaching the Gospel. They can be priests or brothers.

Francis was born into a wealthy family in 1182 and lived in Assisi, Italy. His full name was Francesco di Pietro di Bernardone. As Francis grew up, he began to have visions from God. He decided to give up his wealthy life and lead a life of service and simplicity instead. He encouraged others to do the same and to follow Jesus. He soon started the Franciscan Order and preached all over the world. He loved to spend time in nature and with animals. He had a special love for all of God's creatures.

In 1224, two years before he died, it is believed that Francis experienced the stigmata. The stigmata are the same scars that Jesus received when he was crucified. Francis died in 1226 and was declared a saint in 1228.

CHAPTER 5

It's a Miracle!

Carlo was buried in a tomb in the St. Francis Basilica in Assisi. It is where Saint Francis of Assisi—one of his favorite saints—is also buried.

Soon after Carlo died, the Diocese of Assisi asked the Vatican to recognize Carlo as a saint. Carlo's family owned a second home in Assisi and Carlo spent a lot of time there. When Carlo was visiting, he went to daily Mass and became friends with priests and nuns, so he was well known in that diocese. Everybody who encountered him said they could tell just how special he was. Many believed Carlo was already a saint walking among them. But there are still many steps to becoming a saint.

The Catholic Church began to research if Carlo deserved to be called a saint. They looked through all of his personal belongings and journals to make sure he was as holy as everybody said. They looked at his computers and reviewed his emails. They checked out the different websites he created on the Internet.

They also talked to the many people who knew Carlo. The investigation lasted for years. Everywhere they looked and everything they heard proved Carlo had lived an exceptional and holy life.

Carlo's mom also began receiving emails and letters from all over the world. People told her that after praying to ask her son for help, a miracle happened to them. Some very sick people who were expected to die reported getting better after asking Carlo to pray for them from heaven. The pope needed to verify these miracles. That means the Catholic Church needed to investigate them and declare that they did indeed happen, and that they happened because of Carlo's prayers.

On July 5, 2018, Pope Francis signed a decree, or statement, saying that Carlo lived a life filled with faith, hope, and charity, in a truly unique, or special, way. The declaration

STEPS TO SAINTHOOD

The steps to be named a saint in the Catholic Church are called the canonization process. There are four steps in order to become a saint.

1. The person must be deceased for five years or more, unless there is an exception made by the pope. People from the person's community make a formal request to the bishop of the diocese where the person died, asking for him or her to be named a saint. People who knew the candidate are asked to attest to the person's goodness, holiness, and devotion to God. If this step is passed, the person is then called a Servant of God.

2. The bishop then sends a formal request to the Congregation for the Causes of Saints at the Vatican. This committee of religious people studies the candidate's personal writings, speeches, and the events of that person's life. Once it is confirmed that the person is good and virtuous, he or she is then called Venerable.

3. The next step is called beatification. A miracle must occur, and the candidate must be given credit for the miracle. All miracles come from God, but the saints in heaven can ask God for miracles and intervene on Earth in a special way when people ask them for help. This is what getting credit for a miracle means. If the miracle is approved, the candidate can now be called Blessed.

4. Once the person is called Blessed, a second miracle must occur. Once the second miracle is approved, the person is officially canonized or called a Saint. The pope will honor this saint in a special Mass.

allowed Carlo to be called Venerable. This meant that Carlo was an amazing spiritual person to follow as a role model.

"Carlo's witness indicates to today's young people that true happiness is found by putting God in first place,"[14] the Pope said.

Carlo's mother and father were so honored that their son was on this path toward sainthood. They always knew Carlo was special, but they didn't know how special. Many people were praising them and telling them what a remarkable job they had done raising their son. But Antonia and Andrea didn't think they should be given this credit.

"I don't consider myself as good as Carlo was; but of course, I tried my best to raise my son," explained his mother. "I gave him the freedom

Pope Francis (b. 1936)

Pope Francis is the 266th pope of the Catholic Church. He became the pope on March 13, 2013.

Pope Francis was named Jorge Mario Bergoglio when he was born in Buenos Aires, Argentina. His father was an accountant and his mother was a stay-at-home mom. Jorge grew up always wanting to take care of the poor and to live his faith and some good moral rules—but my husband and I didn't really need to give him much. He did it all."[15]

On November 14, 2019, Pope Francis credited Carlo with a miracle. The miracle occurred in 2013. It was the healing of a seven-year-old boy in Brazil named Mattheus, who was born with a pancreas that did not work correctly. The pancreas is a gland in the body near the stomach. It helps digest food. But Mattheus' pancreas would not let him eat solid food. If he did try, he would get sick. He survived on a liquid diet. The priest in Mattheus' church wrote to Carlo's mother. She sent the priest a relic, one of Carlo's T-shirts.

the needy. He was a kind and thoughtful boy. He became a priest in 1969 and did most of his ministry in Buenos Aires. When he was named the pope in 2013, he chose a new name, Francis, for Francis of Assisi, his favorite saint. He admired Francis of Assisi, just like Carlo. Pope Francis is the first pope in history to be from the Americas. He is also the first Jesuit pope.

Pope Francis is a humble man who still cares very much for the poor. He tries to unite people. He encourages people to talk out their differences. He also preaches the importance of taking care of our planet and our environment.

Like Carlo, Pope Francis wants to share God's message of peace with the world using all forms of modern communication.

"Find new ways to spread the word of God to every corner of the world,"[16] he said.

The priest invited people to come to the church to touch Carlo's T-shirt and to pray for Carlo's help. Mattheus did just that.

On the drive home from church, the boy told his mother he was feeling better. He went home and had a meal of steak, French fries, rice, and beans. After he ate, he did not throw up. Mattheus was miraculously healed. Mattheus' mother took her son back to the doctors. They were puzzled. They could not believe that he was suddenly well.

Mattheus' mother talked about this miracle that happened to her son. "I realized my testimony [story] would give hope to other families,"[17] she said.

Carlo's life of good deeds continued to help in other ways too. His eucharistic miracle website thrived even after his death. It now consists of 150 panels, or boards. Each board shows where one miracle occurred and tells the story behind that miracle. The website can be read in more than seventeen different languages. Italian priests Raffaello Martinelli and Angelo Comastri helped take Carlo's plan one step further. They turned Carlo's work into a live exhibit by printing the website panels onto poster boards. The exhibit has now been displayed on five continents in more than ten thousand parishes.

Relics

A relic is an object that was owned by a holy person (like a thread from their clothing), or it may even be a part of their body (such as a fragment of bone or hair). Relics help us connect to the saints and pray for their help. When we remember a saint's physical presence because of a relic, it reminds us of his or her spiritual presence with us. It is usually something we can touch. The word relic comes from the Latin word *reliquiae*, which means "remains." Many churches have relics that are kept in special places of honor called reliquaries.

One of the Catholic Church's most famous relics is the True Cross. According to legend, Saint Helen, the mother of Emperor Constantine, discovered the actual cross on which Jesus was crucified. Today some churches around the world have pieces of wood believed to be from the True Cross.

Praying before relics or reverencing them (often by kissing the reliquary in which they are kept) is another means of strengthening our faith in the presence of God and the help of the communion of saints.

"As I look around at all these posters this young man, this fifteen-year-old boy created, it brings me to tears," said Robert Ball, a parishioner at St. John the Evangelist in Pawling, New York, where the exhibit was displayed in 2020. "He was able to reach out to millions of people and really help to change their lives."[18]

Before Carlo died, he had started to plan another exhibit. He wanted to create a 156-part series on the places where Mary appeared around the world. He did not live long enough to complete this, so his mother did it for him. This exhibit has also traveled the world and has its own website.

CHAPTER 6

Heading Toward Sainthood

After the miracle of the boy in Brazil was credited to Carlo, the next step to sainthood was the beatification ceremony. Beatification comes from the Latin word *beatus*, which means "blessed." This is the third of four steps toward sainthood. After the ceremony, Carlo would then be called Blessed Carlo Acutis. Once a person is called Blessed, people can officially say prayers in his or her name. The Blessed also gets a feast day. Carlo's day is October 12, the anniversary of his death.

In October 2020, Carlo's tomb was open for people to visit at the Basilica of St. Francis of Assisi. A basilica is a large and important Catholic church. The word comes from a Greek term meaning "royal house."

Carlo's body was displayed in a special coffin for nineteen days, and people came to honor him. Carlo's tomb was white stone and glass so people could see him. Crowds stood in long lines to pay their respects and to pray the Our Father or say other prayers. Children blew kisses at his tomb as they passed.

Carlo had died fourteen years earlier. But, with the help of makeup, Carlo's face and body looked similar to when he was alive. He was dressed in Nike sneakers and jeans and a sweatshirt. These had been his favorite clothes. He also had a rosary wrapped around his hands.

"In some ways, his earthly face was seen again," Archbishop Domenico Sorrentino of Assisi explained. "But his face—let us not forget—by now does not point to [Earth], but to God."[19]

On October 10, the day of the beatification ceremony, thousands of people came to Assisi to honor Carlo. The church was filled. Great crowds watched on giant screens that were set up in courtyards across the city. Millions more watched on live feeds across the entire world. Carlo's mother and father sat in the front row of the church. Many of Carlo's childhood friends attended. People sang and applauded as Carlo was beatified.

"Having a friend who is about to become a saint is a very strange emotion," said Mattia Pastorelli, who had known Carlo since they

were five. "I knew he was different from others, but now I realize just how special he was. I watched him program websites. He was truly an incredible talent."[20]

Carlo's tomb was closed on the night of October 19. Over forty-one thousand people had visited his tomb and prayed for Carlo's help when he was displayed. Once the tomb was closed, it still remained in the church. This way, visitors can still pray there.

48

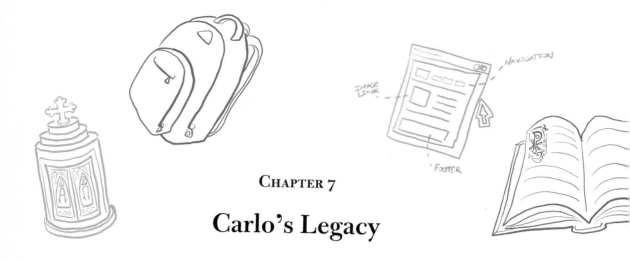

CHAPTER 7

Carlo's Legacy

The final step to sainthood is canonization. This is when the Blessed officially becomes a saint. In order for this to happen, the Blessed must be credited with one more miracle. The time between beatification and canonization varies greatly. Carlo's mom Antonia is hopeful that her son's canonization will happen in her lifetime.

While Carlo waits for sainthood, he continues to spread his messages on Earth. Youth centers across the world have been dedicated in his name. A virtual school in Ontario, Canada, was named in his honor.

"It gives our students hope and inspiration that they too can follow in the footsteps of a holy person,"[21] the Director of Education at the Ontario school said.

If you search for Carlo's name on the Internet, you will find millions of results. There are many documentaries and videos about him on YouTube. There are also social media pages dedicated to him. Although Carlo wouldn't have wanted all this attention, he would be honored that his message—about getting Jesus out to the world using the Internet—is

49

A PRAYER FOR CARLO

This is the official prayer asking God for Carlo's canonization.

Oh Father, who has given us the ardent testimony of the young Blessed Carlo Acutis, who made the Eucharist the core of his life and the strength of his daily commitments so that everybody may love You above all else, let him soon be counted among the Saints in Your Church.

Confirm my faith, nurture my hope, strengthen my charity, in the image of young Carlo who, growing in these virtues, now lives with You.

Grant me the grace that I need (Mention your request here).

I trust in You, Father, and your Beloved Son Jesus, in the Virgin Mary, our Dearest Mother, and in the intervention of Blessed Carlo Acutis. Amen.

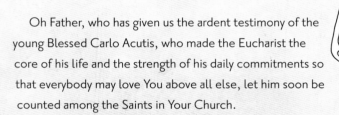

being shared with millions of others. When Carlo does become a saint, some people hope he will become the patron saint of the Internet. He is a modern messenger of God, an example of holiness for our times.

"Carlo used the Internet in service of the Gospel, to reach as many people as possible," said Cardinal Agostino Vallini at Carlo's beatification ceremony. "Carlo saw the web as a place to use responsibly without becoming enslaved."[22]

Carlo's legacy of work with the poor also continues. A new soup kitchen is opening in Assisi. It will be named in Carlo's honor.

Carlo was an only child when he was alive. His mother and father were not able to have any other children. But in 2011, his mother and father had twins, Francesca and Michele. They were born on October 12, the same day that Carlo died. Carlo's mother is sure that they are a gift from Carlo. She thinks it was the sign Carlo promised to tell her that he is in heaven. And like Carlo, his sister and brother go to Mass and pray the Rosary often. Michele also picks up garbage

wherever he goes, just like his brother did. Antonia believes the twins have a mission to continue their brother's work.

Carlo is on the path to sainthood because he led a holy and selfless life in his short time on Earth. He was always looking toward God instead of daily human matters. He was wise and spiritual beyond his years. He wasn't self-righteous. This means Carlo didn't think he was better than anybody else, and he didn't judge those who saw the world differently than he did.

He thought anyone could make the impact he did. This is the real reason why millions of people still look up to him. Even though Carlo was special, he didn't do anything that we all can't do in our own lives. He had a simple formula: he went to church and prayed the Rosary every day. He was good to others. He took care of the environment. He helped the poor. He shared his skills by creating an exhibit about the Eucharist for all the world to see. He was convinced that good things can come through the Internet.

All saints are holy, but young people today can't always identify with those who lived centuries ago. They lived in such different places and in different times. Carlo seems like he could have been anybody's friend. Carlo can be a saint that people today understand and relate to.

"Everything he did, you can do—honestly," said Father Will Conquer, a missionary in Cambodia who has written about Carlo. "And that is what gives us all a lot of hope."[23]

Carlo's words, actions, and computer work can inspire us. Each of us can see ourselves in Carlo. He is what holy looks like in the twenty-first century. And he was able to share his holiness and his beliefs with the whole world.

"Carlo is just a dude with his computer and his love of God," said one admiring teenager. "And that stuff's cool."[24]

A Prayer to Blessed Carlo Acutis

Lord Jesus, you inspired Blessed Carlo Acutis to love you with his whole heart. Because of his love for you, he was able to make a difference in the world during his short time on Earth. He cared for his friends, his family, the poor, and the environment. Light my heart on fire with the same love he felt so that I can make a difference in the place I live today.

Blessed Carlo Acutis trusted in the good that could be done through the Internet and modern technology. Lord Jesus, teach me how to use these tools to bring light and joy to others the way he did. Give me the grace to make good choices and use them with moderation. May the Internet and other technologies help to build people up and bring them closer to you, my God.

Lord Jesus, you know how much Blessed Carlo Acutis loved you in the Eucharist. Show me how to love you there. Never let me forget that you are really, truly present at every Mass and in every church. Through the prayers of Blessed Carlo Acutis, may the Eucharist become my highway to heaven too. Amen.

Learn More About Carlo

Cruz, Joan Carroll. *Eucharistic Miracles and Eucharistic Phenomena in the Lives of the Saints.* Charlotte, North Carolina: Tan Books, 2010.

Kunnappally, Ephrem. *Highway to Heaven.* Kerala, India: Pavanatma Publishers, 2020.

Occhetta, Francesco. *Carlo Acutis: The Servant of God.* Gorle, Italy: Editrice Velar Publishing, 2018.

Websites

Carlo's Eucharistic Miracle Site

http://www.miracolieucaristici.org/.

Carlo's Miracles of Mary Site (Completed by his mother, Antonia)

http://www.themarianapparitions.org/.

Official Website

http://www.carloacutis.com/.

Acknowledgments

Writing a book about a saint can be an intimidating job. After all, saints are the people closest to God that we know. Saints are our messengers, healers, and helpers from heaven. Blessed Carlo taught me, though, that I should not be frightened to write about him. He was just a kid who aspired to live the holiest and best life he could in the short time he had on Earth. And he hoped to inspire other children to do the same. Blessed Carlo believed in the importance of helping people. I certainly would never have been able to write his biography without getting help and guidance from others too.

First and foremost, I would like to thank Carlo's family, especially his mother, Antonia. It amazes me that I was able to reach out and communicate with the family of a saint. The family's secretary, Isabel Reyes, was instrumental in facilitating our communication. We were also so thankful the family was extremely generous in allowing us permission to use photographs and images from Carlo's life (see official website). I would also like to thank Bishop Robert J. Baker. He led me to Carlo's family and also helped me find other wonderful resources. Additionally, I'd like to thank the fifth and sixth grade classes of St. Andrew's School in Newtown, Pennsylvania, for helping us decide on some wording in the book!

It was truly a privilege to write about Blessed Carlo Acutis. I will be forever grateful.

Notes

1. Pope Francis, *Angelus*, October 11, 2020, http://www.vatican.va/content/francesco/en/angelus/2020/documents/papa-francesco_angelus_20201011.html. Papal comments made after angelus.

2. Marie Fazio , "An Italian Teenager Could Become the First Millennial Saint," *The New York Times*, October 12, 2020, https://www.nytimes.com/2020/10/12/world/europe/millennial-saint-carlo-acutis.html.

3. Mathilde De Robien and Cecilia Zinicola , "What Carlo Acutis' Nanny Taught Him—and Us," *Aleteia*, November 7, 2020, https://aleteia.org/2020/11/07/what-carlo-acutis-nanny-taught-him-and-us/?fbclid=IwAR08GUkfYeX208Lh8iWqbRe9iG6iowt5UKj1jyBaQWoiRx-d1JZzblip7IQ.

4. Jesús V. Picón, "Carlo Acutis' Principal: He's a Beacon for Children and Young People," *Aleteia*, October 27, 2020, https://aleteia.org/2020/10/27/carlo-acutis-principal-hes-a-beacon-for-children-and-young-people/.

5. Steve Jobs, "2005 Commencement Address at Stanford University," (June 12, 2005), https://news.stanford.edu/news/2005/june15/jobs-061505.html.

6. Sabrina Ferrisi, "Carlo Acutis Always Lived in the Presence of God," *National Catholic Register*, June 27, 2020, https://www.ncregister.com/features/carlo-acutis-always-lived-in-the-presence-of-god.

7. Paola Bergamini, "Witness Carlo Acutis: 'Nothing More Than Lifting Your Gaze'," http://archivio.traces-cl.com/ (Traces Communion and Liberation International Magazine, vol. 18, is. 2), February 1, 2014, http://archivio.traces-cl.com/2014/02/nothingmore.html.

8. Ephrem Kunnappally, *Highway to Heaven: A Spiritual Journey through the Life of Blessed Carlo Acutis* (Kozhikode, Kerala, India: Atma Books, *Pavanatma Publishers PYT* 2020), 25.

9. Ibid., 31.

10. Courtney Mares, "Blessed Carlo Acutis' Doctors Recall His Last Days in Hospital," *Catholic News Agency*, October 16, 2020, https://www.catholicnewsagency.com/news/blessed-carlo-acutis-doctors-recall-his-last-days-in-hospital-55243.

11. Corinna Turner, "Carlo Acutis: His Life and Legacy," *Catholic Herald*, October 9, 2020, https://catholicherald.co.uk/carlo-acutis-his-life-and-legacy/.

12. Mares, "Blessed Carlo Acutis' Doctors Recall His Last Days in Hospital."

13. *Blessed Carlo Acutis, The Tech Teen Who Found Jesus,* YouTube video, 22:07 (EWTN Home Vaticano, 2020), https://www.youtube.com/watch?v=YUOgYiw_OZ0.

14. Pope Francis, Angelus, October 11, 2020. Papal comments made after angelus.

15. Bree Dail , "Mother of Soon-to-Be Blessed Carlo Acutis: 'Jesus Was His First Priority'," *National Catholic Register*, February 27, 2020, https://www.ncregister.com/interview/mother-of-soon-to-be-blessed-carlo-acutis-jesus-was-his-first-priority.

16. This quote is often attributed to Pope Francis, but cannot be traced to any papal documents or addresses.

17. CNA Staff, "The Miracle Attributed to Carlo Acutis' Prayers," *Catholic News Agency*, October 10, 2020, https://www.catholicnewsagency.com/news/the-miracle-attributed-to-carlo-acutis-prayers-95939. A version of this story was first reported by ACI Digital, CNA's Portuguese-language news partner. It has been translated and adapted by CNA.

18. *The Tech Teen Who Found Jesus*, YouTube video 9:50.

19. Christine Rousselle, "Millennial and Gen Z Catholics Love Carlo Acutis. Here's Why," *Catholic News Agency*, October 9, 2020, https://www.catholicnewsagency.com/news/46147/millennial-and-gen-z-catholics-love-carlo-acutis-heres-why.

20. Courtney Mares, "Beatification of Carlo Acutis: The First Millennial to Be Declared Blessed," *Catholic News Agency*, October 10, 2020, https://www.catholicnewsagency.com/news/46167/beatification-of-carlo-acutis-the-first-millennial-to-be-declared-blessed.

21. Paula Ducepec, "New Virtual School Named for Carlo Acutis," *The Catholic Register*, November 11, 2020, https://www.catholicregister.org/ysn/ysn-news/item/32362-new-virtual-school-named-for-carlo-acutis.

22. See Cardinal Agostino Vallini, *Mass with the Rite of Beatification of Carlo Acutis*, October 10, 2020, https://www.facebook.com/vaticannews/videos/1054120795042904/.

23. Marie Fazio, "An Italian Teenager Could Become the First Millennial Saint."

24. Christine Rousselle, "Millennial and Gen Z Catholics Love Carlo Acutis. Here's Why."

Ellen Labrecque is a children's book writer who lives in Bucks County, Pennsylvania, with her husband and two kids. She has written over 100 books for children on everything from sports to outer space. This is her first book for Pauline Books & Media, where she is also a children's book editor. Additionally, just like Carlo, Ellen loves animals. She has the best writing partner in the world in her dog, Oscar!

Dan Wegendt is a graphic designer, animator, and all around creative guy. He grew up in Youngstown, Ohio, and started making things at the ripe old age of five. His early creative endeavors involved paper, tape, and LEGO bricks. When he discovered that it was someone's job to design cereal boxes, he knew he had found his calling: to be a graphic designer! He and his loving wife, Meghan, live outside of the bustling city of Atlanta, Georgia.

Who are the Daughters of St. Paul?

We are Catholic sisters. Our mission is to be like Saint Paul and tell everyone about Jesus! There are so many ways for people to communicate with each other. We want to use all of them so everyone will know how much God loves us. We do this by printing books (you're holding one!), making radio shows, singing, helping people at our bookstores, using the Internet, and in many other ways.

VISIT US AT WWW.PAULINE.ORG

BOOKS & MEDIA

The Daughters of St. Paul operate book and media centers at the following addresses. Visit, call, or write the one nearest you today, or find us at www.paulinestore.org.

CALIFORNIA
3908 Sepulveda Blvd, Culver City, CA 90230 310-397-8676
3250 Middlefield Road, Menlo Park, CA 94025 650-562-7060

FLORIDA
145 S.W. 107th Avenue, Miami, FL 33174 305-559-6715

HAWAII
1143 Bishop Street, Honolulu, HI 96813 808-521-2731

ILLINOIS
172 North Michigan Avenue, Chicago, IL 60601 312-346-4228

LOUISIANA
4403 Veterans Memorial Blvd, Metairie, LA 70006 504-887-7631

MASSACHUSETTS
885 Providence Hwy, Dedham, MA 02026 781-326-5385

MISSOURI
9804 Watson Road, St. Louis, MO 63126 314-965-3512

NEW YORK
115 E. 29th Street, New York City, NY 10016 212-754-1110

SOUTH CAROLINA
243 King Street, Charleston, SC 29401 843-577-0175

VIRGINIA
1025 King Street, Alexandria, VA 22314 703-549-3806

CANADA
3022 Dufferin Street, Toronto, Ontario, Canada M6B 3T5 416-781-9131